TOP TIPS:
EN(OURAGING FAITH
TO GROW

Ruth Hassall and Piers Lane

© Scripture Union 2008
First published 2008, reprinted 2010
ISBN 978 184427 321 8

Scripture Union, 207–209 Queensway, Bletchley, Milton Keynes, MK2 2EB, England
Email: info@scriptureunion.org.uk
Website: www.scriptureunion.org.uk

Scripture Union Australia
Locked Bag 2, Central Coast Business Centre, NSW 2252
Website: www.scriptureunion.org.au

Scripture Union USA
PO Box 987,Valley Forge, PA 19482
Website: www.scriptureunion.org

Scripture quotations are taken from the HOLY BIBLE, NEW INTERNATIONAL VERSION, (NIV), © 1973, 1978, 1984 by International Bible Society. Used by permission of Hodder & Stoughton, a division of Hodder Headline Ltd. All rights reserved.

Scripture quotations marked (NLT) are taken from the Holy Bible, New Living Translation, © 1996. Used by permission of Tyndale House Publishers, Inc, Wheaton, Illinois 60189. All rights reserved.

The right of Ruth Hassall and Piers Lane to be identified as authors of this work has been asserted by them in accordance with the Copyright, Designs and Patents Act 1988.

British Library Cataloguing-in-Publication Data.
A catalogue record of this book is available from the British Library.

Printed and bound in Singapore by Tien Wah Press Ltd

Logo, cover design, internal design: www.splash-design.co.uk

Internal illustrations: Colin Smithson

Typesetting: Richard Jefferson, Author and Publisher Services

Adviser: Alison Hendy

Scripture Union is an international Christian charity working with churches in more than 130 countries, providing resources to bring the good news about Jesus Christ to children, young people and families and to encourage them to develop spiritually through the Bible and prayer.

As well as our network of volunteers, staff and associates who run holidays, church-based events and school Christian groups, we produce a wide range of publications and support those who use our resources through training programmes.

CONTENTS

INTRODUCTION

John Westerhoff, a leading thinker on issues of faith development, wrote a book entitled *Will Our Children Have Faith?*. This question is increasingly being asked by parents and church leaders, with the follow-on questions of, 'So how do we help them develop a relationship with God?' and 'At what age are children capable of faith?' Over recent years, much has been done to raise the importance of children's and youth ministry within churches, which is wholeheartedly welcomed. However, one by-product of this seems to be that in some ways the church has convinced parents that their children's ministry is responsible for the spiritual formation of a child so that parents may find themselves unsure about the part they have to play in encouraging faith.

Our belief is that the spiritual formation of a child takes place within the home *and* the church community. Through this book we aim to help all those involved in walking alongside children and young people on this journey of faith. Primarily, we will explore how churches can help those accompanying children and young people to encourage faith through the everyday things of life, not just the intentional teaching times. Faith, after all, is a gift from God, and he has chosen to reveal himself through his world and his Word. Sometimes children are actually better equipped to see this than adults are. Our prayer is that as we journey together with the children around us, we will all grow in our awe and wonder of who God is and how he is at work in his world and his people.

WHAT THE BIBLE SAYS ABOUT ENCOURAGING FAITH

What is faith?

First of all, we need to look at what we mean by faith. As people, made in the image of God, all of us are spiritual beings. We need to understand that spiritual formation begins at birth, if not before (Psalm 139), and although this formation may not necessarily be positive, it will happen.

One dictionary definition of faith is 'allegiance to a person or a cause, or a strong belief in something, especially without proof.' The writer to the Hebrews, however, aims to convince his readers that faith is rational and based on sound evidence. Mindless faith doesn't come into it! He writes: 'faith is being sure of what we hope for and certain of what we do not see.' (Hebrews 11:1)

In her book, *Touching the Future*, Gill Dallow writes that faith is the framework in which our spirituality grows – we have faith in something or an allegiance to someone which then guides our spiritual formation. For the purpose of this book, this is the definition that we're using, whilst also recognising the Hebrews' definition of faith.

When we asked people the questions, 'When were you first aware of God?' and 'When did you come to a point of faith in Christ?', we found that most people had an awareness of God long before they came to a point of what they would call 'personal commitment'.

This reflects what faith development theorists would say. There are a number of different theories on the ways in which faith grows but the two leading theorists are John Westerhoff (mentioned in the introduction) and James Fowler. Westerhoff's model is based on the assumption that people go through four different stages on the way to a commitment of faith:

Stage 1: Experienced faith – what we experience of other people's faith and its effects on their lives helps us to form our own faith.

Stage 2: Affiliative faith – activities, experiences and feelings create a sense of belonging to a faith community.

Stage 3: Searching faith – a personal faith develops from questioning and looking at possible answers.

Stage 4: Owned faith – affiliative and searching faith combine to give a secure personal faith which can take account of other viewpoints – often described as a conversion experience. This level of faith is God's intention for all.

The important basis of this model is that rather than being a list of stages that we move through, it's more like the rings of a tree, with each ring adding to and changing the tree, yet building on what has already grown.

Let's apply this to the life of a child to see how it works. Children's first experience of faith comes from those around them: parents and the faith community. If this is a good experience, the likelihood is that they will move into stage two where they feel very much part of that community. As they grow, and particularly as they reach early adolescence, there will often come a time of questioning, of asking the difficult questions, such as, 'Do I believe this because it's true or because it's what I've always been told?' This highlights the need to allow space for young people to ask questions and express their doubts, not simply to dismiss them. Such doubts are real and therefore necessary if a young person is to move onto stage four – the point of owned faith. Here they discover faith isn't just the faith of their family, or those around them, but is intrinsic to who they are and how they live. The God of their family is their own personal God.

Although this book is primarily about working with children and young people, it may be helpful to apply these stages to adults attending a course that explores Christian faith. People with little or no Christian experience attend, and their first experience of faith is the people of faith they meet there. If they feel welcomed, they are likely to come back the next time. After a few weeks a sense of belonging is formed. They may not feel they agree with all that's being said, but they definitely want to be known as part of the group. Then comes a time of searching, asking questions, working out what Christian faith would look like in their life and encountering God through prayer. This hopefully leads to 'owned' faith.

Think about...
Have you been part of an adult discipleship course? How far do these four stages apply to any of the people who came?

It can also be helpful to think of faith as being made up of three parts:

Faith as believing – knowing what we believe and learning foundational truths. This combines receiving knowledge with believing it.

Faith as relationship – relating with the one in whom and about whom we believe.

Faith as action – being able to put into practice what we believe.

Children need the opportunity to experience all three of these elements, and they have a capacity for all three, although each element will look different at different ages.

The early years

According to Francis Bridger, author of *Children Finding Faith*, the foundations of faith are laid early and involve learning to trust. Significant, trustworthy adults in a child's life are in a position to enable a child to trust God. Awe and wonder is a key feature in the lives of under 5s and is a great way to introduce them to the Creator God who loves them.

Lower primary years

Fantasy can still seem as real as real life – Santa and Jesus happily co-exist. However, it's at this age that children start to take on the ideas of significant adults. Karen Marie Yust wrote in *Real Children, Real Faith*, 'Young children have two important strengths operating for them as they learn about the world and their role in it: keen observational powers and imagination… They "try on" roles and behaviours of people and characters with which they are familiar.'

Upper primary years

A child's ability to distinguish between fact and fiction is fairly well developed and they are keen to question. They will want to know how we know that the stories of Jesus are true, and are ready to see that what we believe has an impact on how we behave.

Over 11s

For many young people it's no longer enough to simply accept things because they know the people who are telling them. They need to work it out for themselves.

From generation to generation

Throughout the Bible there is the recurring theme of one generation telling the next about what God has done. Psalm 78 is just one example of this: '… we will tell the next generation the praiseworthy deeds of the Lord, his power, and the wonders he has done. He decreed statutes for Jacob and established the law in Israel, which he commanded our forefathers to teach their children, so that the next generation would know them, even the children yet to be born, and they in turn would tell their children. Then they would put their trust in God.' Psalm 78:4–7

Again in Deuteronomy 6:7 the command there is to 'impress them [the commandments] on your children. Talk about them when you sit at home and when you walk along the road, when you lie down and when you get up.'

Commands like these assume that children can have a relationship with God and that the evidence of this is seen in changed behaviour in everyday living as well as intellectual assent.

Often we will find that the Damascus road experience of Paul is held up as the normal experience of how people come to faith. But in reality relatively few people come to faith in a dramatic moment; it's more of a journey. In *Conversion in the New Testament: Paul and the Twelve*, Richard Peace explores the differences between Paul's experience and the experience of the disciples who model a gradual coming to faith in Jesus. In the Bible we see that faith is actually a whole way of life that grows as we travel life's journey.

The home and faith development …

In the Old Testament the home is the primary place for faith development.

'Tie them [God's laws] as symbols on your hands and bind them on your foreheads. Write them on the door-frames of your houses and on your gates.' Deuteronomy 6:8,9

Wherever family members went, they would bump into the Law of the Lord. It would be all around them, woven into the fabric of everyday lives. Being the people of Israel was their identity and anyone born into a Jewish family took on that identity. Parents and family members took seriously the command to pass on the stories of God's people throughout the generations so that children would know that they too were part of that story. God, who did these amazing things, was their God and could be trusted in all situations.

Obviously our situation is different! In many ways we live in two cultures: the secular world around us, and the Christian community to which we belong. Our challenge (as it was for believers in the New Testament) is to find ways for our homes to be full of God's story so that it's all around us, and known through the things that we do together.

The role of the Church

In the Bible almost all children belonged to a faith community. Times of worship and scheduled festivals were at the heart of community life, with children at the centre. In the Passover celebration, children asked the questions that prompted the retelling of the story of God's act of deliverance.

In *Will Our Children have Faith?* John Westerhoff writes, '...a community is a group of people who have shared life together and have stories of that life together ... If our children are to develop good memories of their early life in a faith community, they must have chances to share life with the faith community.'

Sadly, in many churches, people's attitudes to children and faith can be like Jesus' disciples: 'Then little children were brought to Jesus for him to place his hands on them and pray for them. But the disciples rebuked those who brought them. Jesus said, "Let the little children come to me, and do not hinder them, for the kingdom of heaven belongs to such as these."' (Matthew 19:13,14)

Of course there is value in children sometimes learning separately from adults. But compartmentalising church life often means that children are excluded from a large part of corporate worship. Also, because of limited time available we have become bound up in 'educating' children in the 'knowledge' of the Bible and Scripture, to the detriment of helping children grow to understand about and experience God's love in action. They may not experience the church as a caring community, where people enjoy being with each other and learning from one another. As John Westerhoff wrote, '... when our churches segregate children from the rest of the community we stunt the spiritual formation of the entire community.'

Of course we need to teach children biblical truths. However, if our limited time with children is focused on teaching in a 'schooly' educational way, we will fail them. We need more time to help them apply what they are learning to their lives, to show them how one story fits into the context of the whole Bible and how the Bible can become a guide for life. We need time to respond to God in worship together and time for fun together!

We need to sometimes let children take the initiative so that they are helping adults to learn and grow in their faith. There has to be a strong link between church and home, so that what is taught at church is brought to life in the fabric of everyday living.

This calls for churches to actively set up occasions when the whole family of God can come together to have fun and celebrate God's goodness.

A change of heart

The Bible clearly supports the view that children can grow in faith. God's intention is that children should be raised within the community of faith, never knowing a day lived without the awareness of God's presence and involvement in their lives. However, that isn't where it ends. There does need to come a point where children own the faith of their family and their faith community for themselves – knowing that the God of their family and their faith community is their God and that they love him and want to continue following him throughout their life. As Paul wrote, 'For you are not a true Jew just because you were born of Jewish parents or because you have gone through the Jewish ceremony of circumcision. No, a true Jew is one whose heart is right with God. And true circumcision is not a cutting of the body but a change of heart produced by God's Spirit.' Romans 2:28,29 (NLT)

Children need to be given opportunities to respond to God

personally, but not in a pressurised way. We need to be sensitive to the fact that the way a child voices their response might look very different from how an adult would voice it. We need to give children opportunities to keep saying 'yes' to God and recognise them as the people of God even if they can't make an eloquent statement of faith.

Ron Buckland's picture in *Children and the gospel* is of how children (particularly from Christian families) come to faith. He believes that rather than a child either being in relationship or not being in relationship with God, having faith in God is more of a spiral journey, working towards the centre. Throughout our lives we're either taking steps closer to the centre or further away from it. Somewhere within the spiral is a line that we cross, which could be called 'owned faith'. As parents and children's workers, our role is to keep helping children take steps towards the centre.

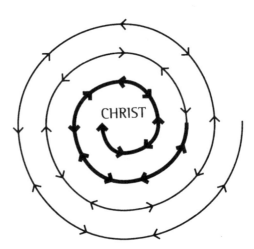

SOME BASIC PRINCIPLES

Children have innate responses to the world around them. These can be summarised as **play**, **learn** and **explore**. So, for example, if a young child is given a toy, they will first play with it – using their imagination to answer questions such as, 'Can this be fun?', 'What can I do with it?', 'Does it hold my attention?' At some point playing will develop an element of learning, trying to relate and make sense of it personally – 'What is this?', 'If I drop this, will it break?', 'If I bang this on the table, will it still work?' At another point in the activity, the toy will be further explored – 'What are the possibilities for this object?', 'What can it become?', 'What is there still to discover?'

Children also use playing, learning and exploring in their relationships with other people. Often relationships are formed around play, but learning will take place when difficulties emerge, or when a playmate is no longer available – 'Will they still be my friend tomorrow?', 'Will I see them again?' At other points the relationship will be explored – 'What can we do together?', 'What can this friendship become?'

In our model, play, learning and exploration are the keys to developing faith, and they overlap. The three approaches share a relationship which is illustrated by this diagram:

Each part of the shape is only created by drawing others. If the pen is kept on the paper after the first 'circuit' is completed, each part of the shape is traced over and over again. In a similar way, faith develops through play, learning and exploration – by tracing and retracing the overlapping experiences of faith.

Playing

A child's world is full of new experiences, and the response of the secure, growing child is to engage with these new experiences through play.

Francis Bridger in *Children finding faith* says that play 'enables us to explore and express emotions, to act out and resolve disturbing aspects of life, to achieve desires and ambitions beyond the scope of ordinary life and to create new worlds of meaning'. In a word, play is vital.

Playing with the whole idea of what it means to trust in God gives children:

- The permission to encounter God at their own level of maturity
- The opportunity to use their imagination
- The interaction with others that will reinforce the importance of sharing faith with others
- A way of answering the question, 'Is this engaging or enjoyable?'

The key question to ask here is, 'Is this engaging or enjoyable?' If the answer is 'Yes', it is possible for faith to develop out of their positive experience.

Learning

Learning takes place through success and failure, when things work, and when they don't. Children not only play with the world but they put the world to the test. A child learns about the world in various ways. For example: they may throw food on the floor to see what response they will receive; they may ask endless questions; they may jump down from an increasing number of stairs; they may ignore a friend they will later rely on; they may ask questions that include the possibility of disappointment and reappraisal.

Think about...
Does your church help children to play with and enjoy faith? How? If not, why not? How can you help children or young people use play to encounter God in your Sunday sessions?

Through this the world is evaluated and absorbed, acquiring knowledge as well as applying such knowledge to life's experience. It is what is known in education circles as both learning *about* something and also learning *from* it. As those who are called to walk with children and young people on their way into faith, we need to grasp the importance of this and to facilitate it in a supportive and secure environment – even when we do not necessarily have all the answers.

Learning about faith in creative ways gives children:
- The ability to check if something is safe or reliable
- The ability to choose between options
- The capacity to trust beyond sight
- A way of answering the question 'What do I learn about God?'

The key question to ask here is, 'What do I learn about God?' Sometimes the answer will be obvious and easy; sometimes more difficult and unsettling. Yet supporting children as they imaginatively

Think about...
How does your church help children to creatively ask questions about faith? In what ways does your church help children apply the answers to these questions to their personal experience?

learn about their faith is vital, as it will provide foundations for the future.

Exploring

Exploration of the world around us, whether it is the natural world, the world of education and learning, or the world of relationships is vital for children. Exploration may come after learning but in many ways it precedes it. There is an overlap. Exploration is also part of play but the exploration that we are considering here is the ability to venture beyond the initial experience to something more.

Exploration gives children:

- Ideas of what something can become or develop into
- Knowledge of the value of exploration
- A hunger for learning and discovery
- The ability to avoid complacency or dullness
- A way of answering the question, 'So what now?'

Think about...
How does your church help children to explore their faith? How can we help children explore their world to discover God at the centre of it?

Our key question here is, 'So what now?'. Christian faith needs to be developed. It is not stationary. This development must be done through exploration, not simply through education. Children need to find ways of asking questions about where faith will lead them.

Exploring the three questions

We have seen that playing, learning and exploring are at the heart of faith development. We have outlined what we mean by these words, and have tried to indicate how important it is for children to respond. We have also established that it is important to ask the following key questions:

- Play – is this engaging?
- Learn – what do I learn about God?
- Explore – so what now?

These questions might be asked (although they may not necessarily use these exact words!) in a variety of situations on behalf of children or by children themselves. For example, when encountering a Bible story children and young people should be able to ask 'Is this engaging?' and answer positively because of how the story has been presented. They should be able to ask what they have learnt about and from God, and should also be able to explore where the Bible story takes them, to find out about their own relationship with God or other people through what they are reading, hearing or seeing.

This play, learn, explore approach and the key questions are not restricted for use in a church setting. For example, when shopping with the family, a child could see the fun in going shopping but also learn something about the character of God as Creator or Provider. They might then explore what it means to be a consumer or think about the effect of their purchase on other people. This will help develop faith that is not just for church or Sundays, but for everyday life.

Another example might be when watching a football match, children and young people identify with the fun of the experience, but could be encouraged to learn that God made our bodies to be strong and wants us to do well at different things. They could then explore the importance of playing fairly.

Of course, sometimes the questions will have negative answers – something might not be fun or apparently engaging. Life is full of disappointments and doubts. We will fail children and young people at the first hurdle if we do not provide them with the tools to cope with this, standing with them, with honesty and compassion, using the Bible and prayer. Faith is not always easy; God is indeed a mystery; the path ahead is sometimes hard to find and needs to be searched out. Such tough experiences, if embraced rather than avoided, are vital and productive. It is worth noting that many young people who know Jesus are often better equipped than many of their peers to account for pain, loss and disappointment.

In reality…

Two teenage sisters joined the youth group and were discovering what faith meant. Then their father committed suicide. They had endless questions as they tried to make sense of their faith in the light of what had happened. The youth worker was a great support.

Belonging

'Expressions of faith will only be real if we treat children as part of the church community now, and not as outsiders who will one day become full members. Only then will they grow in faith.' *Touching the Future* Gill Dallow

Churches have a number of ways to define the membership of a church, ranging from a tight adult membership to broadly embracing anyone of any age associated with activities run by the church. Children and young people can be seen just as the church of the future, not the present. Or they may be seen as a vital part of the church family now whose contribution is valued and whose need for spiritual nurture and care are catered for on every level. Page 28 explores this further, but we would want to stress that children play a vital part in the church now, as their faith grows.

> **Think about...**
> How does your church welcome new people? How are new followers of Jesus welcomed? What about babies, young children and young people?
> What messages are given about what it means to belong to God's family?
> What are the signs that children are recognised as being the church of the present as well as the future?

3 PRA(TI(AL IDEAS

In a nutshell, John Westerhoff's answer to the question, 'Will our children have faith?' is that they will, if the adults in their lives accompany them on their spiritual journey to provide them with opportunities to experience the life of faith at home and in the faith community. However, there will be children and young people in clubs, youth groups and churches whose significant adults do not have a faith in God to share. As far as is possible, the faith community must take responsibility for the spiritual nurture of such children and young people.

A framework for faith to grow

In order for faith to grow in any of us, not just children or young people, churches and families need to provide opportunities for the following:

- Worship – the whole of our lives are to be lived in worship to God. Here we're specifically talking about time alone, or with others, to tell God how amazing he is.
- Believing – opportunities to hear and learn the stories of God and how he's at work in people's lives.
- Witness – to tell others how God is at work in our lives, and share the good news of Jesus.
- Service – using gifts and talents that God has given us to serve others and build up the church.
- Belonging – a community where everyone can feel accepted and has a role to play.

Taking each of these key areas of discipleship, we will apply to them the model of play, learn and explore and the three key questions. We will look at how faith can be developed at church (within the faith community), at home and in the world around us. The suggestions are by no means exhaustive. Think of further ideas of your own to try out!

Worship

In church

Encourage children to participate in the music group, by singing, playing an instrument, operating the OHP or data projector or preparing PowerPoint slides.

Is this engaging? Hopefully so!

What do I learn about God? God gives people different gifts. Here is something I can do with others or on my own.

So what now? I can continue to use the gifts I have to help others worship God and to do so on my own.

At home

A church can encourage families to hold creative family prayer times, by giving parents ideas and resources and assuming this as the norm. Families where only one parent is a Christian or where there are other factors that make faith development a challenge, will need additional support and encouragement.

Is this engaging? If done with help and enthusiasm.

What do I learn about God? There are too many possibilities in this context to mention!

So what now? Once I'm used to talking with God and leading prayers naturally at home, I could lead prayers in a different situation.

In the wider world

Go for a walk to comment on what you see in a Sunday session – as a church family event or for individual families to do themselves.

Is this engaging? Probably!

What do I learn about God? An opportunity to marvel at what God has created.

So what now? I can make a habit of appreciating God's world.

Believing

In church

Within Bible teaching sessions make sure there is a time for children and young people to respond to what has been taught.

In reality…

The group of 11 to 14s were keen to look at the book of Revelation. In week two, they explored the letters to the seven churches in chapters 2 and 3. In small groups the leaders asked them to reflect on what would be written in a letter sent to *their* church, bearing in mind the pattern of the Revelation letters – an encouragement, a warning and a promise. When the groups got back together to read out their letters, almost every group had written the same thing about the church. This was used to challenge the church's priorities.

Is this engaging? If it's well thought about and interactive, engaging different senses other than hearing.

What do I learn about God? Looking at the Bible helps me focus on and hear from God.

So what now? I will expect to hear from and respond to God as I read the Bible.

At home

Read the Bible together as a family.

Is this engaging? There are many resources to help families read the Bible together (see page 32). Churches can help families by providing suggestions and material to follow up issues after a service.

What do I learn about God? God has given us his Word, and we can learn about him and how to live in a way that pleases him.

So what now? Children are equipped to hear from God for life.

In the wider world

Go to the cinema as a church or family group. Talking about a film after seeing it takes the experience a step further. For example, ask questions like, 'What did you think about the way the character handled a particular situation?' or 'What do you think God would say to them?'

Is this engaging? Yes.

What do I learn about God? God has things to say about current issues, using different forms of communication.

So what now? What I believe affects how I react to activities I do with my friends, which can strengthen my faith.

Witness

In church

Give children an opportunity in services and their groups to share what God has been doing in their lives.

Is this engaging? Probably even though it may be a bit scary. Adults may have far more hang-ups about this than children naturally do!

What do I learn about God? He can use my story to encourage other people. I am also inspired by the stories and behaviour of others.

So what now? I can look for other opportunities to share my story.

At home

Pray regularly for friends who don't know God.

Is this engaging? Yes, but we need to be persistent.

What do I learn about God? God is interested in me and my friends and wants us to know him.

In reality...

During the Easter holidays we hold a children's holiday club. A few weeks before the club all the children in church are given two invitations – one for themselves and one to give to a friend. In the children's groups we talk and pray about who they might invite. I'm always amazed at how seriously they take this. It really matters to them that their friends come. After the holiday club we continue to pray for their friends by name.

So what now? Answers to prayer encourage more prayer.

In the wider world
Keep a record of friends prayed for, either as a diary or in a family prayer postbox.

Is this engaging? Yes, but we need to be persistent.

What do I learn about God? God wants everyone to know he loves them.

So what now? I need to look out for opportunities to share Jesus with others.

Service

In church
Children and young people take part in welcoming people to church, being part of the prayer team, caring for the church grounds or premises, photocopying the notice sheet, organising a collection for a world in need.

Is this engaging? It could be – think of ways of making it so.

What do I learn about God? In God's family we all need each other. I can help others as a way to please God.

So what now? In what other ways can I serve others?

At home
Perform a regular job in the home such as loading the dishwasher, baking a cake for a special occasion or emptying the bins.

Is this enjoyable? It can be and especially if done with others.

What do I learn about God? I need to serve others even though I may not always want to.

So what now? It feels good to help others and think of others. What else can we do?

In the wider world
Visit a neighbour who is elderly or unwell.

Is this engaging? If we're honest, this isn't always fun, but it's definitely beneficial.

What do I learn about God? He wants to comfort those who are lonely or sick, and he does that through us.

So what now? What else can we do?

Belonging

In church
Celebrate some Bible festivals together such as Passover or Pentecost or work to make something significant out of baptisms or thanksgiving services.

Is this engaging? Most definitely.

What do I learn about God? God wants us to intentionally remember what he has done for his people in the past that affects what we expect him to do now.

So what now? I must not forget what God has done for his people, in the past and now.

At home
Look at photo albums of your family over the years, and tell the stories of family members. This could include mission partners supported by the church.

Is this engaging? Yes.

What do I learn about God? God's people make up a huge family, of which our family is part. We belong together.

So what now? I have a role to play in God's larger family.

In the wider world

Take an active interest in a project that cares for those in need.

Is this engaging? Yes, and challenges complacency.

What do I learn about God? God cares for those who suffer and we can be his means of making a difference.

So what now? The world's need is inexhaustible, so there is plenty to be involved in for the rest of life!

We could give many more ideas, ways of getting into the Bible, or great resources to find, buy and use. But ultimately, it's not just the things that we do, it's the way that we see and use them which enables every moment to become a faith-developing opportunity.

Whilst parents have the primary role in helping children grow in faith, the church has an important role in encouraging parents in their awesome responsibility. It falls to the church to think how they can be truly inter-generational so that people of all ages find a place to belong, and to provide opportunities for families to engage in worship together.

'The church's ministry to children is broken. A cursory look doesn't reveal its brokenness. From the outside children's ministry looks healthier than ever. But it is broken… It's broken when we teach children the Bible as if it were just another book of moral fables or stories of great heroes. Something's broken when we trivialize God to our children. It's broken when we exclude children from perhaps the most important of community activities: worship. It's broken because we've become dependent on an 18th century schooling model, forgetting that much of a child's spiritual formation is affective, active and intuitive. It's broken when we depend on our programs and our curriculum to introduce our children to God – not our families and communities. It's broken when we've come to believe that church has to be something other than church to be attractive to children. It's broken when we spend lots of money making our churches into playlands that entice children to God through food fights and baptisms in the back of fire trucks. And perhaps most importantly, it's broken when the church tells parents that its programs can spiritually nurture their children better than they can. By doing this, we've lied to parents and allowed them to abdicate their responsibility to spiritually form their children. A church program can't spiritually form a child, but a family living in an intergenerational community of faith can. Our care for our children is broken and badly in need of repair. Let's imagine together a new way, a new future.'

Ivy Beckwith, *Post-modern Children's Ministry*

'Praise God, he is present and at work in the playground as well as the pew, and invites us to join him wherever the real dance is! And if there's one thing that children know better than anyone it's that!'

Keith White *Exploring Child Theology Keynote paper for the Archbishop's Council's Strategy for Children Forum, 10th March 2004*

Our hope is that this book has challenged you to mend the 'brokenness' of your children's and youth ministry so that their faith can grow strong.

TEN TOP TIPS

1. See the whole of life as an opportunity for faith development.
2. Recognise the importance of relationship building.
3. Affirm the family as the primary place for faith to grow, but work hard at creating links between home and church.
4. Don't be scared of hard questions or always having to have the right answer – 'I don't know, let's find out together' can be a very effective response.
5. Offer support to families where it may be tough to nurture faith and support to those whose families are unable to nurture faith, for whatever the reason.
6. Always allow time for a response when teaching is taking place in church.
7. Look out for the non-scheduled teachable moments, and opportunities for celebration – thanking God for his goodness and provision.
8. Encourage all family members to keep growing in faith. We are all on this journey.
9. Remember the stages of development and have appropriate expectations.
10. Memorise the three key questions and use them anywhere and everywhere!

RESOURCES

Ivy Beckwith, *Postmodern Children's Ministry*, Zondervan, 2004
Francis Bridger, *Children Finding Faith*, Scripture Union/CPAS, 2000
Ron Buckland, *Children and the gospel*, Scripture Union, 2001
Karen Marie Yust, *Real Kids, Real Faith*, Wiley, 2004
David Staal, *Leading Kids to Jesus*, Zondervan, 2005
David Staal, *Leading Your Child to Jesus*, Zondervan, 2005
Hands On Bible, Tyndale, 2004
Gill Dallow, *Touching the future*, BRF, 2002
Kathie Reimer, *1001 Ways to Introduce Your Child to the Bible*,
    Broadman and Holman, 2002
Family Activity Organiser, Scripture Union, 2008 – an annual product –
    see inside back cover
Richard Patterson, *Families with faith – Survival skills for Christian
    Parents*, Scripture Union, 2006